THE PROBLEM WITH NIGERIA

BY DR. DAMINABO SONNY BRIGGS

Email: lillianclinic@yahoo.com

Tel: 08033383908, 08056090359

Published in Nigeria by
Osia Digital Press
8 Owhonda Street, Diobu
Port Harcourt, Rivers State, Nigeria
Tel: 08033128938, 08037055272

ISBN: 978-978-52709-2-1

DEDICATION

This book is dedicated to all patriotic Nigerians who clamour for peace, unity, equity and justice!

____

**In loving memory of
my mother, Madam Lillian
Saturday Jack,
(Nee Lilly-Tariah)
1925-2010**

____

CONTENTS

The book, 'The Problem With Nigeria,' by Dr. Daminabo Sonny Briggs, is an x-ray of Nigeria's foundational problem. Perhaps, driven by passion and a burning fire of patriotism, the author, like the late Prof. Chinua Achebe, delves into the scary, daunting task of diagnosing Nigeria's perennial socio-economic and political ailments and discovers that the root cause of the nation's woes is the structural defect of its foundation.

In the author's view, the Nigerian ship can never be steered aright, irrespective of the expertise and pedigree of whoever is piloting it, as long as the nation keeps floating on a foundation that remains structurally defective. This is how he puts it: *"The problem with Nigeria is the fault in its structure. There is nothing significant any super human can do in leadership. Even if we bring Angels from Mars, Jupiter or Neptune to rule us, no significant progress will be made with the present way Nigeria is constituted."*

He believes that it is this structural fault in Nigeria's foundation that gave birth to the avalanche of vices ravaging the country.

The work could be described as a continuum of Achebe's treatise: *'The Trouble with Nigeria'*, because of the similarity of the titles and subject matters discussed in both works. The only difference is that while Achebe harped on the problem, Briggs discovered its root cause and suggested ways of tackling it, thus giving the Nigerian government a clue in its bid to solve the problem and reposition the country. The author believes that until this structural defect of Nigeria's foundation is corrected, the cobra-like monster called corruption, and its plethora of poisonous tentacles ravaging the country, such as greed, poverty and impunity, among others, will never be eliminated.

The author reflects on the crude oil discovery and exploration in Nigeria and regrets that rather than be a blessing to the country, like in other climes, the precious mineral has become a curse, especially to the people of Niger Delta Region, because of the pollution its exploration has caused in the oil producing communities as well as the general under-development, neglect and suffering the people have been subjected to by both the government and the oil companies.

The author, no doubt, is a patriotic Nigerian who is very passionate about the country's future and how to make it bright hence he makes suggestions on how the various problems confronting the country can be tackled.

The book, therefore, becomes a handy tool for the Federal Government as it aims to take Nigeria to the promised land of socio-economic and political development through President Goodluck Jonathan's transformation agenda.

It can also serve as a guide for the delegates participating in the ongoing national conference, as recommendations are made by the author on how the country can take advantage of the conference to address its multifarious problems.

Moreover, *The Problem With Nigeria* can equally be an important guide for both the present and future generations of Nigeria as it offers an insight into how the nation should be run to actualize the visions of our founding fathers. I, therefore, recommend it to every Nigerian.

Sir Opunabo C. Inko-Tariah (JP)

INTRODUCTION

When in 1983, Late Professor Chinua Achebe, of blessed memory, wrote his famous book entitled "The trouble with Nigeria" in far away Kano State, a young medical Doctor serving his country in the National Youth Service Corps, in a far remote village, Ikot Ekpo, in Akwa Ibom State, in the same year, wrote his manuscripts that eventually gave birth to a riveting novel entitled "AZ Mafia: The Namerian Experience", in 2002.

That young Doctor is Dr. Daminabo Sonny Briggs!

Reading through these two books, one can easily and undoubtedly see the similarities in the content, substance or messages embedded in them.

———————————— x ————————————

It would appear as if one mind wrote the two books! This is not surprising to me because we wrote about the chaos, the rot, the injustice prevalent in the society, with a view to proffering solutions. The coincidence is just the timing. I can safely say, without equating my humble self to a super literary Icon as Late Professor Chinua Achebe that my "AZ Mafia: The Namerian Experience", is a novel version of "The trouble with Nigeria".

The affinity my first novel, "AZ Mafia: The Namerian Experience" has with Late Professor Chinua Achebe's book, "The trouble with Nigeria", has driven me into further research on the Nigerian situation.

In his book, the Professor wrote, and I quote:
> **The trouble with Nigeria is simply and squarely a failure of leadership. There is nothing**

basically wrong with the Nigerian character. There is nothing wrong with the Nigerian land or climate or water or air or anything else. The Nigerian problem is the unwillingness or inability of its leaders to rise to the responsibility, to the challenge of personal example which are the hallmarks of true leadership.

I totally agree with the erudite Professor on the above quotation and all what he said in his book. But on further analysis of the Nigerian situation, it is my well-considered opinion - and I have thus come to the conclusion- that the <u>failure of leadership in Nigeria</u> is as a result of <u>the structural defect of the Nigerian foundation;</u> and that this defect has given birth to a colossal cancerous monster or octopus called <u>political corruption</u>, which, in turn, has yielded a multitude of malignant tentacles, feasting on the soul of Nigeria. They include:

- Greed
- Impunity
- Extreme poverty
- Poor remuneration
- Disparity in salaries
- Over bloated bureaucracy
- Unitary system
- Section 308 immunity clause
- Non-declaration of assets
- Absence of effective deterrence
- Weak institutions
- Skewed distribution of Local Government Areas (LGAs)
- Skewed distribution of resources
- Election rigging and violence
- Attitude of condoning corruption
- Culture of sharing and wastefulness
- Manipulation of census figures

1

THE STRUCTURAL DEFECT

The problem with Nigeria is the fault in its structure. There is nothing significant any super human can do in leadership. Even if we bring Angels from Mars, Jupiter or Neptune to rule us, no significant progress will be made with the present way Nigeria is constituted.

In a multi-ethnic and multi-religious conglomerate as Nigeria, the best suited political arrangement for us is Federalism in its real sense. This was what our great founding fathers agreed to practise in post independence era, which brought about healthy positive competitive spirit and real development to the then three Regions of the North, West and East.

The military intervention dislodged the lofty policy of Federalism, and introduced a unitary structure, which was in keeping with their training, but inimical to the well-being and unity of the country.

The Regions made a lot of progress because of the practice of True Federalism. The groundnut pyramids in the North, Cocoa in the West, and coal and palm produce in the East brought much needed resources, and therefore development, to their respective regions.

The structure we are operating currently is Federalism on paper, but unitary in practice. This is the crux of the matter. Unitary system is an anathema to a nation that is multi-ethnic. It breeds disaffection and disunity among the citizenry, generates conflicts, do-or-die politics and terrorism, and promotes corruption in all its ramifications. The centralization of enormous power at the Centre, as occasioned by the unitary system, breeds infighting and desperation to be in charge of affairs. Such desperation eventually leads to massive rigging of elections, violence and assassinations.

This is quite understandable as "Ogas on Top", with their supporters, control the huge resources at their disposal, be it at the Federal, State or Local Government level. No wonder we are having, and will continue to have major intra-and inter-party upheavals as to who controls the "almighty" Centre!

The unitary system encourages the doctrine of sharing the national cake, without any consideration of how to bake the cake!
Nigeria is not likely to make appreciable

progress in our march towards actualization of Millennium Development Goals (MDGs) if we continue with this sharing propensity. Imagine the practice of Governors going to Abuja every month, cap in hand, to collect their shares. It is obvious to any thinking mind that this method cannot be sustained forever. The source of the money, which is oil, will finish one day, as in Oloibiri, where oil was first struck in 1956! What are we going to share when we get to that stage? Will the country disappear?

The prediction that Nigeria will disintegrate in 2015, or thereafter, came from an American. I don't believe that Nigeria will disintegrate, if by that they mean one section of the country taking up arms to fight the rest.

But Nigeria can still collapse if we continue with this massive sharing without baking, which inexorably leads to massive corruption and monumental wastages. This is economic suicide!

How do we then heal the structural defect? The honest and true answer is for us to adopt Federalism, not only on paper but also in practice. We should be patriotic enough to divide Nigeria into six geo-political Regions or zones of North East, North Central, North West, South South, South East and South West. These should constitute the Federating units.

The 36- State structure should be subsumed within the regions. Each Region or zone should be autonomous, that is, it should be free to man its resources and pay tax to the Federal Government. This will not only rekindle positive competitive spirit as seen in the First Republic when groundnuts, cocoa and palm produce and coal developed their respective regions, but will also bring about real development of the nation.

Local Government is not supposed to be a third tier of government in a Federal system. Hence, the 774 LGAs, and any others that may be created, should operate directly under the States or Regions. Each Region or zone will be free to create as many States and LGAs as feasible, and states and LGAs so created will solely be funded by the Regions or Zones, and not by the Federal Government. This arrangement will eliminate the monumental injustice as glaringly seen in the skewed and lopsided distribution of States and LGAs.

The restructuring suggested here allows or permits equity, fairness and justice to all segments of the Nigerian population. Each of the six geo-political regions has enough resources to fund its development, as Nigeria is blessed, not only with oil and gas, but innumerable solid minerals scattered or naturally distributed evenly within the country. Moreover, oil is being discovered not only in the South East, but gradually also in the Middle Belt, as well as up North.

The tax to be paid to the Federal Government by the six Regions or zones will form a formidable pool from which zones or regions in dire need will stand to benefit.

I predict, as Nostradamus would do, that Nigeria, in no distant time, will join India and China to send rockets into outer space, if we are sensible enough to restructure the country along these lines, mentioned in this book!

2

POLITICAL CORRUPTION

The problem with Nigeria is obviously the faulty structure, leading to structural imbalance. The structural imbalance promotes political corruption, and the political corruption, in turn, fuels the imbalance.

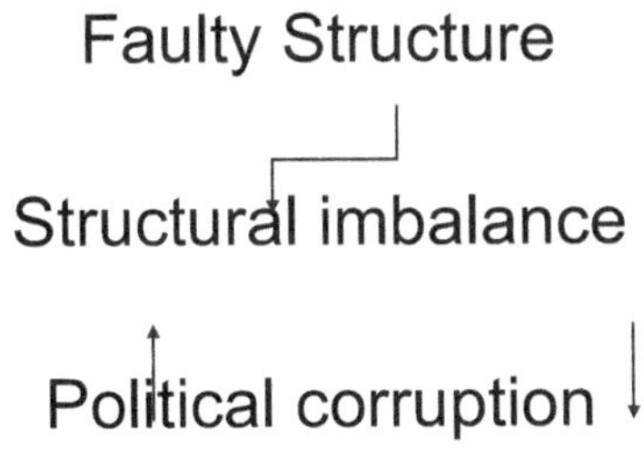

Faulty Structure

Structural imbalance

Political corruption

This unhealthy, inharmonious and destabilizing relationship between the faulty structure and political corruption is the problem with Nigeria. The combination breeds disequilibrium in the system, and until this cycle is broken and dealt with, Nigeria will not enjoy peace, development and stability.

The subject of corruption was discussed in my earlier book entitled "How to fight corruption in Nigeria". Here, it is only essential to reinforce the fact that corruption is the major obstacle to our growth and development, and also to state that it is the root cause of the insecurity we see in the country.

There is no country in this world that is immune to corruption. The emphasis in this chapter is on political corruption, which is the mother of all corruption.

Political corruption, as stated earlier in my previous book, occurs when politicians and political decision-makers, who are entitled to formulate, establish and implement laws for the benefit of the people, are themselves corrupt. It also occurs when policy formulation and legislation are tailored to benefit politicians, legislators, their cronies and ethnic regions.

It is political corruption that fuels the system whereby 70 to 80% of our annual budget is earmarked for recurrent expenditure, leaving little for capital projects. It is political corruption that supports very few individuals earning millions of Naira per month as take home pay, with free armoured cars to boot, while majority of Nigerians go hungry without jobs or die quietly. It is the same political corruption that supports and maintains skewed distribution of resources, and lopsided distribution of States and Local Government Areas (LGAs).
All these are happening in a country that God has blessed with abundant human and natural resources. So blessed that we don't suffer from

volcanic eruptions, tsunamis, tornadoes, hurricanes, typhoons, cyclones and other natural destructive forces!

Political corruption swallows up trillions of dollars from oil, and recently, gas revenues, without any commensurate palpable development.

Hear what fellow Nigerians and others said or are saying about corruption in Nigeria:

- Prof. Osundare

  "If we don't kill corruption, corruption will kill Nigeria"

- Femi Falana

  "Corruption seems to have become the fundamental objective and principle of public policy"

- Prof. Akindele Oyebode on Judiciary

  "The lady of Justice, Themis, who is

supposed to be blindfolded with a sword on one hand and scale on the other, peeps through in Nigeria to really see who is before her…."

- Bishop Matthew Kukah
"Corruption, sad as it may sound, is the only thing that works in Nigeria."
- Tony Marinho of The Nation Newspaper
"Corruption devalues every government naira to 30 kobo"

- The National Orientation Agency (NOA)
"That Corruption is now more contagious than HIV/AIDS, and it is a threat to Nigeria's corporate existence as a Nation."
- The United States Consul General in Nigeria, Jeffrey Hawkins, speaking during a courtesy visit to Punch Nigeria Ltd. in Magboro on 5th December, 2012, identified corruption as a key element hindering the country from

attaining its full potential. He said:"The potential of the people of Nigeria is absolutely phenomenal….but this potential is not being harnessed because of the potential risk element of corruption in the polity…"

☐ Mr. Bill Clinton, former United States President, at the 18th Thisday Newspaper Awards, held at the June 12 Cultural Centre, Abeokuta, Ogun State, alerted our leaders that Nigeria is frittering away its oil revenues: "you haven't done well with your oil money".

☐ Former President of Ghana, Jerry Rawlings, called on African Countries, especially Nigeria, to fight Corruption head-on now or risk a sudden eruption as occurred in Egypt and Tunisia (Arab Spring)…while giving a keynote address at the 2nd Zik Lecture series of the Faculty of Social Sciences, Nnamdi Azikiwe University, Awka on the theme: "Eradicating Corruption in Africa…." March 8,

2013.

To put corruption in Nigeria in its proper perspective, compared to other nations of the world, we need to look at studies carried out by various International Bodies:

1. **Transparency International (TI)**
This is a Berlin-based Global Civil Society Organization, leading the fight against corruption. It publishes its report annually, ranking the countries of the world according to the degree to which corruption is perceived to exist among public officials and politicians.

Nigeria's record of Corruption Perceptions Index (CPI) scores has been totally and annoyingly disappointing, since 1996. We are always rated within the bottom group in almost all surveys.

In the 2012 TI Corruption Perceptions Index (CPI) Scores, Nigeria was ranked 139 out of 176 countries, with a CPI score of 27 out of 100.

In sub-Saharan Africa, Botswana was ranked the best, 30 out of 176, with a CPI score of 65.

Cape Verde, the best in the West African region, ranked 39 out of 176, with a score of 60.

Ghana ranked 64 out of 176 with a score of 45. Nigeria ranked the 3rd most corrupt country in the West African Region, coming behind smaller and poorer countries such as Cape Verde, Ghana, Liberia, Burkina Faso, Benin, Senegal, Gambia, Niger, Sierra Leone, Mauritania, Togo and Cote d' Ivoire

In the 2013 TI CPI scores, Nigeria was ranked 144 out of 177 countries, with a score of 25 out of 100, making us one of the most corrupt countries in the world.

Denmark and New Zealand were the cleanest in 2013, scoring 91 out of 100. Botswana was cleanest in Africa in 2013, with a score of 63 out of 100, and ranked 30th in the world. In West Africa, Ghana was the Star in 2013, garnering 46 points out of 100, and ranked 63rd in the world.

2. **<u>GLOBAL COMPETITIVENESS INDEX (GCI) FOR 2010 - 2011 BY WORLD ECONOMIC FORUM</u>**

Ranked Nigeria 127th out of 133 countries, relying on criteria such as electricity supply, infrastructure deficit, accountability, macro-economy health/education, technological readiness and business sophistication/ innovation.

Same study within the African continent, ranked Nigeria 25th out of 35 nations covered, coming behind smaller and very poor countries such as:

- ☐ Ethiopia
- ☐ Rwanda
- ☐ Gambia
- ☐ Benin
- ☐ Botswana
- ☐ Cameroon
- ☐ Tanzania
- ☐ Swaziland

GLOBAL COMPETITIVENESS INDEX 2012-2013 BY WORLD ECONOMIC FORUM

Ranked Nigeria 115th out of 144 countries, i.e., at the last bottom 30.

Top ten countries dominated by European countries - Switzerland, Finland, Sweden, Netherlands, Germany, United Kingdom...

Ghana	-	105th position
South Africa	-	52nd position
Gabon	-	99th position

Significantly, Nigeria still lagged behind South Africa, Botswana, Cameroon, Kenya and Ghana.

3. **THE 2011 HUMAN DEVELOPMENT INDEX (HDI)** released by United Nations Development Programme (UNDP), placed Nigeria 156 out of 187 countries. This ranking was based on education, income and life expectancy, i.e., quality of life index.

   MO Ibrahim Foundation provided more damaging indices, coming from a black African!

4. **THE 2010 IBRAHIM INDEX OF AFRICAN GOVERNANCE SURVEY** ranked Nigeria 40th out of 53 African Countries.

The Ibrahim Index featured 17 criteria, some of which were:

Personal safety: Nigeria ranked   -   34 out of 53

Lack of infrastructure   - 39 outof53

Accountability/corruption   -   34 out of 53

Health/Welfare   - 43 out of 53

Education: Nigeria ranked   -   32 out of 53

Human Development   - 42 out of 53

TOP 10 COUNTRIES FOR THE AFRICAN GOVERNANCE SURVEY (YEAR 2010).

1st Position   -   Mauritius

2nd Position   -   Seychelles

3rd Position   -   Botswana

4th Position   -   Cape Verde

5th Position   -   South Africa

6th Position   -   Namibia

7th Position   -   Ghana

8th Position   -   Tunisia

9th Position   -   Egypt

10th Position   -   Lesotho

The 2012 Mo Ibrahim African Governance Survey ranked Nigeria 43rd out of 52 African Countries, excluding Sudan and South-Sudan. (40th out of 53 countries, in the year 2010).

The greatest challenge facing us, as patriotic Nigerians, is how do we uproot the cancer of corruption in the polity? I have good news for fellow Nigerians, if only we are willing to accept it! The way we have been fighting corruption is faulty! But the fault is not coming from incumbent President or past Presidents, or even the police or the legislature or judiciary. Not even the Economic and Financial Crimes Commission (EFCC) or the Independent Corrupt Practices and other related offences Commission (ICPC)! Even if we bring Angels from heaven or outer space to run the Nigerian state as presently constituted today, the problems of corruption will not abate, but rather keep multiplying.

This is because the fault is not in individuals but in the system. The problem is systemic.

The architectural design of the Nigerian foundation is faulty, and this is the crux of the matter. And until we are ready to tackle the structural defects, all our efforts to combat corruption in Nigeria will be a waste of time.

These are some of what we need to do to drastically reduce, if not uproot, the cancer of corruption in Nigeria:

- Carry out political restructuring along true and fiscal Federalism
- Elect the right people as leaders devoid of rigging and violence; implementing fully the Justice Uwais Recommendations.

- Reduce wastages and bloated bureaucracy, e.g. collapsing the bicameral to unicameral legislature, thereby halving the total number, and looking at the possibility of paying allowances only (not salaries) to politicians at all levels.

Reducing the wastages will need copying the United States of America (USA). United States of America (the largest economy in the world) has a federal cabinet not exceeding 20. The cost of general administration in the USA is less than 10% of the Federal Budget, compared with Nigeria's 70% to 80%. China and India have the largest bureaucracies in the world, but their average annual expenditure on general administration is only 12%.

- Insist on independent and strong institutions such as:

   Legislature

      Judiciary
      The Press
      INEC
      EFCC, ICPC, Conduct Bureau
      Audit etc.

☐ **Amend Section 308 Immunity Clause**

Section 308 Immunity Clause is a welcome clause as it protects those in governance from unnecessary litigations, which can distract them from performing their duties. But it can also promote corruption, hence there is need to separate criminal from civil cases, and allow it to be operational for civil cases only.

☐ **Declare assets**

Assets should be declared before, during and after leaving public office. The declaration should be in the open and the people should have the right to question such assets.

☐   Effective deterrence
Absence of effective deterrence is one major reason why corruption is multiplying in geometric proportions. Many looters go scot free with their loots.

In China, corrupt officials are severely dealt with.
In Europe and other western countries, the loots are recovered and appropriate punishments served. It is advisable to copy the European methods of dealing with corruption.

FIVE KEY FACTORS IMPEDING NIGERIA'S DEVELOPMENT AS SEEN FROM THE EYES OF RICHARD DOWDEN (DIRECTOR OF AFRICA ROYAL SOCIETY) WHO CAME AS GUEST SPEAKER ON OUR

51ST INDEPENDENCE, ANNIVERSARY, ABUJA, included the following:

- Oil as a curse rather than blessing because of non-investment for future generations
- Corruption linked to oil and others
- Flight of human capital
- Nigeria's Reputation
- Politics

On politics, Richard Dowden said Nigerian politicians are the highest paid in the world. He did not stop there. He gave a figure of Two million dollars per annum take home pay, that is, including salaries and allowances.

Professor Itse Sagay (SAN), a renowned legal luminary, was alleged to have removed the veil of secrecy surrounding the actual take home pay of politicians and members of the National Assembly.

The breakdown, according to the Professor, is as follows:

- A Senator in Nigeria earns N240 million ($1.7million) per annum. A member of the House of Rep. earns N204 million ($1.45million) per annum.
  (We have 109 Senators and 360 members of House of Representatives).

- An American Senator earns $174,000 per annum. UK Parliamentarian earns $64,000 per annum

- Therefore, a Nigerian Senator earns almost 10 times the salary of US counterpart, and more than 20 times the salary of a UK parliamentarian.

- The President of US earns about $400,000 per annum

3
LEADERSHIP

The problem with Nigeria, as earlier stated, is majorly due to the faulty structure in its foundation, which in turn has given birth to or promotes political corruption.

I accept that leadership has a role to play in the polity, whether negatively or positively. The truth of the matter is that a defective political structure is more likely to overwhelm a positive leadership than vice versa.

A committed leadership is expected to be patriotic, selfless, responsible and ready to distribute the dividends of democracy equitably to the greatest number of citizens, irrespective of ethnicity, tribe, sex or religion.

Such leaders are hard to come by! Only very few African leaders have scaled through this hurdle. One very good example is Late President of South Africa, global Icon, Nelson Mandela. Even so in South Africa, restructuring of the polity was a prerequisite for good governance.

Another very good example of love of fatherland and personal example is that of the President of Malawi, Mrs. Joyce Banda, who on assuming office as President, sold the presidential aircrafts, reduced the fleet of cars and cut her salary by 30%! It is this failure of leadership that has prevented Mo Ibrahim, the Sudanese-born British Engineer, from releasing his mouth-watering Awards for good governance in Africa in the last two to three years. In his leadership ranking in Africa, Nigeria has always been in the bottom group.

The problem with Nigeria is more than that of leadership. Those in power are doing their best according to the prevailing circumstances! If one can shift the blame of failure of governance from structural defect and political corruption to anything else, that of "followership" is a more important consideration than leadership. And this is worrisome, and a big challenge! It is a trite saying that the people deserve the leadership they have. The point I am making is that power, ultimate power or sovereignty belongs to the people. And when the people fail or refuse to exercise their rights to good governance, equitable distribution of resources and appointments and other good things of life, the blame game should not be directed to the leadership. It is their good luck!

All through history, "the followership" determines the direction of leadership. This depends on how educated and enlightened the citizenry are. What is the level of literacy in the country? A large proportion of illiterate citizenry is likely to be poverty personified walking on dry thin legs! Such individuals cannot drive leadership; that is why some people conclude that Nigeria is the easiest country to govern! We are the happiest people on Earth, while living in misery and untold hardship. How then can anyone blame the leadership, seeing the acquiescence, gullibility, docility, and even the "siddon look" attitude of the masses?

All these are happening in a country where you have multitudes of egg-heads, iconic figures and professors. In other climes, the youths drive leadership to positive ends without violence. Not so in Nigeria! Many of our youths, in the absence of employment, offer themselves for "hiring and renting" for negative political ends and other nefarious activities.

The problems with Nigeria are multifarious, in declining order of severity: structural defects, political corruption, defects of "followership" and leadership.
What we need to do is to have men and women of integrity, honesty and people with zero-tolerance for corruption to lead us. This will entail among others:

- Restructuring of the polity
- Electing the right people without rigging and violence
- Having independent and strong institutions
- Reducing wastages and bloated bureaucracy
- Enforcing transparency and accountability

4
THE TRAGEDY AND CURSE OF OIL

Some will argue that the problem with Nigeria is OIL! They may be right. When the problem confronting a nation is gargantuan like an "elephant", description of parts of the "elephant" is correct according to one's perspective.

Anti-corruption crusaders have come to the conclusion that eighty percent or so of Nigeria's problems will disappear if our oil dries up as water did on the surface of Mars millions of years ago! This is not hard to believe if we recall the good old days in the country before independence, and in the First Republic before the war, when the regions depended on their agricultural produce, rather than oil.

The gift of oil to any nation is a blessing. Nigeria is the only country in the world where the gift of oil is a curse rather than a blessing. This much was said by Richard Dowden, Director of Africa Royal Society London, who was invited as a Guest Speaker on our 51st Independence, Anniversary in Abuja. In his own judgment, oil is a curse rather than blessing because of non-investment for future generations.

Our oil is a curse because it is seen as free for all, otherwise taken as "No man's property". The resultant effect is that all manner of people within and outside the country, invade the Niger Delta to steal and siphon the crude oil into their private pockets.
Oil is put to good use in other oil-producing States. Revenues from oil are put in Special

Accounts, and only the profit accruing from such deposits is used for development. The special accounts are set aside for future generations, knowing full well that oil does not last forever!

Crude oil was first discovered in Oloibiri, in commercial quantities, in 1956. Today, oil is found in almost every community in the Niger Delta, and some Local Government Areas of the South East, and hopefully some parts of the North.

However, oil is seen as tragedy and curse in most parts of the Niger Delta, including the Ogoni Land. The oil, to the people of the Niger Delta, is expected to generate much needed development and employment in the oil sector. Such developmental needs include connecting bridges and roads to open up the Delta Region, setting up industries in the areas of agriculture and fisheries. The people of the Niger Delta are demanding the development of the Delta region, just as Abuja was developed from virgin forest.

They rightly, point to the abandonment of Oloibiri in its present sorry state after all the oil in its bowels had been effectively drained! Happily, the Federal Government has not abandoned the Niger Delta. Various interventionist Bodies had been set up in times past, from the days before the defunct OMPADEC to Niger Delta Development Commission (NDDC), and Ministry of Niger Delta Affairs.

In spite of the above, palpable development is yet to be seen at the grassroots. The people of the Niger Delta are demanding that even the unfair thirteen percent derivation funds be put into a special account for future generations in the communities. These funds are to be managed by the community representatives, and not by political leaders.

The Petroleum Industry Bill (PIB) is expected to address some of the injustices in the oil sector. The 10% fund to oil-bearing communities is a welcome development, judging the amount of devastation to life and the environment as a result of oil exploitation and exploration. Also, it should not be seen as being too much, as most of the oil blocks in the country are allotted to people from outside the Niger Delta.

The oil is a tragedy and curse to the people of the Niger Delta. This is as a result of widespread pollution of our land, rivers and seas. The pollution is from two sources: leakages from old rusted pipes and sabotage. Studies have shown that majority of the oil spillages are from old pipes that were laid about fifty years ago without effective maintenance.

However, a proportion of the spillages is due to sabotage. Whatever the cause, spillages call for urgent clean-up operations.

The environmental damage in the Niger Delta is unquantifiable as spillages are either denied by oil companies or very little is done to contain such catastrophe. The spill in the Gulf of Mexico, some years back, elicited quick response both from President Obama, and even the oil companies involved. The clean-up was urgently done and commensurate compensation paid to affected persons and communities. This is difficult to achieve in Nigeria. Most of the successful compensatory payments are ordered from oversea courts. Surprisingly, the UNEP Report, ordering the Federal Government to begin clean-up operations in Ogoni land, and begin to pay compensation, has not been implemented three years after! The Movement For the Survival of

Ogoni People (MOSOP), has been blaming the Nigerian Government for delay in its implementation. However, all hope is not lost as efforts are geared towards kick-starting the implementation of the UNEP Report.

The side effects of the spillages are too numerous to mention. The environment is devastated, and may take hundreds of years to fully recover. The land becomes less fertile, leading to very low agricultural yields which may yet become harmful to human consumption. Sea creatures die and disappear, and since majority of people in the Delta are fishermen and women, their economy remains grounded!

At the human level, they breathe polluted air, leading to premature deaths due to respiratory diseases and cancer. The water they drink is contaminated too, leading to higher mortality and morbidity in the Niger Delta, and reduced life span.

The issue of oil theft is a worrisome development in a country where oil is our mainstay of the economy. Out of our daily production of more than two million barrels, about four hundred thousand barrels are stolen! This is as a result of corruption in every sector of the polity, including the oil sector. The theft is continuing because oil is seen as no one's property.

The level of poverty in the land, and the over-powering greed of a few, are fuelling this level of corruption in the oil sector. The magnitude of theft could even be higher than the above quoted figures, as the true quantity of oil produced in the country is not known or overshadowed in official secrecy.

One continues to wonder if the big ships and badges that come to steal or siphon our oil pass through a non-existent "Bermuda triangle" on

5
TRIBALISM/ ETHNICITY/ RELIGION

The title of this short book is "The Problem With Nigeria". Nigeria has a multiplicity of problems, but the title is stressing "the problem" and not "the problems". This is deliberate.

Emphasis is given to "The Problem" which, when tackled, will sort of solve all other problems to their barest minimum manifestations.

The problem is the structural defect in the polity, which has emanated from itself, political corruption. Therefore, "The Problem", as a sown seed, has borne fruit, one of which is tribalism or ethnicity!

What is tribe? What is tribalism? What is ethnicity? Let us refresh our minds. Tribe is defined as a group of people of the same race, and with the same customs, language, religion etc. living in a particular area, and often led by a Chief. Tribalism is defined as behaviour, attitude etc. that are based on being loyal to a tribe. Ethnicity is defined as the fact of belonging to a particular race (All definitions from the Oxford, Advanced Learner's Dictionary)

Late Professor Chinua Achebe, in his book: "The Trouble With Nigeria", succinctly defined tribalism as "discrimination against a citizen because of his place of birth. This definition seems more appropriate and I beg to adopt it!

The use of the word "tribe" appears to be

derogatory in our contemporary world. This could be one of the reasons why traces of the word "tribe" were flung into oblivion in our initial National Anthem:

Though tribe and tongue may differ

We should remember that it is not everything about tribe that is bad. Our mode of dressing, the food we eat, the way we cook, the way we conduct our weddings and burials, all constitute our cultural heritage.

It is now fashionable to describe the tribal groupings as ethnic nationalities. Most of the countries of the world are made of different ethnic nationalities, yet they all live in harmony and unity. Those who live in such blissful relationship do not attach sentiments or emphasis on tribe or ethnicity. The rewards for this patriotism are development, peace and prosperity.

The problem with us is that we are still very much attached to ethnicity. The sins of tribalism and ethnicity have been transferred to "States of origin". That is to say that "statism" has now taken the place of tribalism. This notion is officially supported when we are asked to fill our State of origin, and even our Local Government Area in our National forms. This is the beginning of the discrimination of citizens according to their places of birth.

This brings us to another vexing issue of who is a citizen? Who is an indigene of a particular State or community? Is he the one whose great grandfathers or mothers were from that community?

Is he the one who was born in that community by a settler father or mother? Or is he the settler who has lived in the community for decades and has paid all his taxes for the development of the community?

The settler/indigene dichotomy should be abolished as it has brought a lot of disunity, infighting, bad blood, and even unthinkable and unnecessary bloodshed.

Emphasis and attachment to ethnicity and State of origin have given rise to discrimination in terms of employment, appointments, admission to schools, colleges and universities, unfair and lopsided distribution of resources, and even politics of census and election manipulations!

It is tempting to say that the problem with Nigeria is religion, especially more so when you look at the killings of Christians and Muslims, the burning of churches and mosques. But this can easily be debunked when you consider the fact that for the past fifty years of our existence, the Christians and Muslims and other faiths have been living in peace and harmony, without violence and bloodshed of any kind.

What went wrong?

What is the purpose of religion? Is it not an attempt to reunite us with our Creator, irrespective of the path we choose to achieve reconciliation? That being the case, the tool we need to achieve reconciliation is LOVE, as preached by all faiths. Therefore, LOVE should be the unifying factor, and not divisive, thus driving peace, harmony, unity, kindness and mercy. If we understand this LOVE truthfully, we should not open our doors to violence, hatred and bloodshed which are anathema to the very LOVE we should be imbued with.

Nigeria is a secular state, and this is what should uphold in a mulit-religious setting. One's

6

EMPHASIS ON PAPER QUALIFICATIONS

The problem with Nigeria is illiteracy with its twin brother ignorance. Education is, therefore, the key. The awareness education brings, the knowledge it ensures, the confidence it builds, the empowerment it generates, is the key to solving the myriads of our socio-economic and political problems.

The second of the eight Millennium Development Goals (MDGs) is to achieve universal primary education by 2015. That is to say that all children must have completed primary schooling by the year 2015.

This magic year is barely one year to come, and we are never close to achieving this lofty goal. Many of our children are still out of school, with primary school net enrolment rate of 58% (2008-2011); male youth (15-24 years) literacy rate of 78% (2007-2011); and female youth (15-24 years) literacy rate of 66% (2007-2011) (UNICEF).

In decades past, education in Nigeria was comparable to the best in the world. Time was when lecturers and professors from various regions of the world converged on our universities to teach; time was when students from all over the world came to Nigeria to study in our various universities; time was when almost all admitted students had accommodation in campuses which could be described as spacious, clean, and with toilet facilities comparable to five-star Hotels; time was when we had functional libraries with modern books and journals; time was when our laboratories were well-equipped.

What went wrong?
Where are the expatriate lecturers? I remember the good old days where first class graduates were retained as assistant lecturers. The picture we see today is the adulteration of the academic community with some lecturers who are themselves not qualified as students in those universities or higher institutions they teach.

The reason why this is so is because of corruption in the educational sector, chief among which is the emphasis we place on paper qualifications!

 I recall how I was drafted in December 1972 to teach the final year class preparing for the West

African School Certificate Examination in Elementary Mathematics in Bishop Dimeari Grammar School (BDGS), Yenagoa, now in Bayelsa State. The remarkable fact was that I started the teaching job while awaiting the result of my School Certificate examination I wrote in November 1972. The main hurdle I was faced with was acceptability, on the part of the students, of my ability to handle the subject. I was pleasantly surprised when they threw at me one of the toughest problems to solve as test of my ability. I was more than able to "dismantle" the problem in few seconds, as Mathematics was my best subject. Shouts of approval filled the hall! The final outcome was that most of the students had distinction in Mathematics.

The point being made here is that what is in the head is more important than paper qualifications. Excessive emphasis on paper qualifications is likely to sacrifice merit on the altar of mediocrity. This is the reason why we have fake and "Toronto" certificates, and those that are bought with big sums of money and sometimes "bottom power", circulating widely in our national institutions at all levels, establishments, and even in the National and State Houses of Assembly.

The trend is that those who go as far as buying Degree certificates negotiate for Second Class, Upper Division, the reason being that this class is likely to guarantee them places of employment by oil and major companies. Unfortunately, these oil companies and others are in great error by opening their doors of employment only to those graduates with Second Class Upper Division and higher for further tests and evaluation. In this age and time where examination malpractice reigns supreme in our institutions at all levels, the oil companies and others towing this line of policy should take closer look at the performance analysis of many who score very high marks in the Joint Admissions and Matriculation Board Examination (JAMB) but fail woefully in Post JAMB examinations conducted by various universities.

The right thing to do, if we are to lay emphasis on merit, is to call for applications from all those who have passed their degree examinations, irrespective of class, and let all applicants write a qualifying examination. The idea is to choose the best from the lot. If this is done, it will turn out, just as in cases of JAMB, that majority who will be successful, will not necessarily only come from Second Class Upper Division, and First Class.

Another problem with our education policy is institutionalization of quota system or sustaining dichotomy between advantaged and disadvantaged States in the admission policy. This policy does great harm to merit and it is one of the reasons for the poor standard of education in the country. A situation where a pupil or student who scores 200 out of 400 is denied admission due to higher cut-off point, while, someone who scores 30 out of 400 gains admission, on the basis of coming from disadvantaged States, is the height of injustice and corruption.

The resultant effect is that we admit those who are incompetent and not ready for higher learning into our institutions. What such students are likely to do are not difficult to imagine; intimidation of the academic community, cultism, prostitution, examination malpractice, and outright purchase of degree certificates etc.

All efforts should be made by well-meaning

7
NATIONAL CONFERENCE (NC)

Majority of people, if not all, who have witnessed horrific effects of war, as is currently happening in Syria and other hot zones of the world, will agree to the wise saying:

it is better to jaw-jaw than war-war

There was compelling reason more than ever before, for us to come together to discuss the problems confronting our dear country. This called for National Conference (NC). Credit should, therefore, be given to Jonathan Presidency for convening the National Conference.

The deafening call for National Conference (NC) had been submerged for years.

The need for the NC was overwhelming, considering the chaos in the country with its attendant insecurity. The NC is to address the imbalance in the country as well as the socio-political injustices that stare us in the face!

What we have is a military constitution, which is incapable of righting the political wrongs.

Previous conferences did not see the light of the day because of insincerity of our leaders, and seeming opposition from others. True, one of the previous conferences succeeded to the level of four out of the six zones of the country clamouring for the NC. The fear of others is that the NC can lead to the disintegration of the country, and that the National Assembly is already in place to tackle or take care of the political issues bothering the minds of the various ethnic nationalities.

It is pertinent here to address such fears. It is argued that sovereignty belongs to the people, and that this sovereignty has been handed over to the National Assembly to hold in trust for the people; that we elected the men and women into the Assembly, and so it is their responsibility to act on our behalf.

Many others have argued that the National Assembly members were elected primarily to make laws according to the constitution on ground. They further posit that they are not empowered by law to make a brand new constitution. It is true, however, that they can amend parts of the constitution, but not to make a new constitution.

What Nigeria needs, if we are to remain one indivisible country, is to make a new constitution agreeable to all stakeholders in the country, and that will include all of us, not a constitution suiting a section of the country, but detrimental to other sections or zones.

Some have also argued that the National Assembly, as presently constituted, is very faulty because some of them were selected and not elected. This school of thought argues strongly that the present skewed distribution of Representatives, mainly based on the spread of Local Government Areas (LGAs) in the various sections or zones of the country, is one of the injustices that should be addressed in the NC. Why, they argue, is it possible to continue with the fact that old Kano State (now Kano and Jigawa) having 71 LGAs, presenting preponderance of representatives in the National Assembly over and above Lagos State, for example, having 20 LGAs? The only reason why this anomaly can be sustained is if the population of the old Kano State (Kano and Jigawa) is proportionally higher than Lagos State in the ratio of 71:20, that is almost 7:2. But the reality on ground, judging from the 1963 Census Figures, showed the opposite, and that is, that the population of Lagos State was higher than old Kano State. Even if you take the last Census Figures (2006) in which Kano State (minus Jigawa) is magically said to be more populous than Lagos State, which has not been divided since its creation, it is still hard to accept. This weird ratio of 71 for Kano and Jigawa to 20 for Lagos State cannot stand the test of justice.

Now let me address the fear that the NC is likely to divide the country. This cannot be true! What will divide the country is the refusal to allow the people to come together to fashion out what is agreeable to all sections or zones of the country. The refusal to right the socio-political maladies and wrongs inherent and embedded even in our present constitution, is what is likely to dismember the country.

I can assure all that every reasonable Nigerian wants to live in one united country. Nobody is itching to pull out of Nigeria. The propaganda that Nigeria will split is a deceit. The silent reason why some people are opposing the NC is because they don't want to let go the unmerited and sickening advantages they enjoy over and above other sections or zones. This selfish idea is the force driving some to oppose equity, justice and fair play. Therefore, the status quo should be maintained, so that few continue to enjoy 80% or more of our oil blocks, and deny the Niger Delta People of even 10% to oil-bearing communities!

Many opponents of the NC, just to maintain their obscene advantages, have talked about leaving out contentious issues. Which issues are contentious? Is it that any undue advantage should not be discussed, so as not to address such injustice?

People have also disagreed sharply on whether the conference should be sovereign or not. Whether sovereign or not, the decisions arrived at, at the conference, should not be diluted or doctored by any individual or group of individuals, including the National Assembly. The decisions reached should be implemented for the good and unity of the country. If need be, such decisions or resolutions can be referred to a referendum, possibly assisted by the United Nations.

Some who oppose the NC are likely to tolerate it if there are "no go areas". Why should people talk of "no go areas"? Are we in slavery? Are we not free to discuss matters militating against our survival, if I may ask? There should be no restrictions on what to discuss. The fear that the country will disappear if such is allowed is completely unfounded and misplaced. I see it as camouflage to hide the real reason for the opposition, and that is to continue perpetually the monumental cheating of the rest of us.

Some do not believe that the problems of this country have to do with the structure, form of government and the laws. The problems of this country, as they claim, are as a result of collapse of national ideals, collapse in moral values. I humbly beg to disagree! The problems of Nigeria are originating from this faulty structure of the Nigerian foundation, which has given rise to the said collapse of national ideals, moral values and conscience.

This faulty foundation has given rise to political corruption, which has given birth to twins: a failing state and insecurity.

What are some of the issues that must be addressed amicably if we are to remain in one united and peaceful country, called Nigeria?

1. **<u>FEDERAL OR UNITARY SYSTEM?</u>**

What we are practicing is solely a unitary system. This should be abolished in favour of Federal system. The country should be divided into 6 or 8 zones -- 3 or 4 in the North, and 3 or 4 in the South. The 36-State structure should be subsumed within the regions. Each region should be free to man its resources and pay tax to the Federal Government. This will rekindle positive competitive spirit and lead to real development as seen in the First Republic.

The system of government we are running with 36-State structure plus the Federal Capital Territory, thirty six governors and retinue of commissioners, assistants with a multitude of members in all the State Houses of Assembly, coupled with 774 Local Government Areas with equal number of Chairmen and all the Supervisory Councilors, is not only wasteful, but cannot be sustained for a long time in a mono-economy, soaked in corruption.

The solution to this problem is to restructure the country into six regions or zones with a Central Government. This will reduce the profligacy to the barest minimum, thus releasing funds for actual development.

2.   **BLOATED BUREAUCRACY**

Nigeria is failing because of the bloated bureaucracy and the monumental wastages in operation. Presidential system of Government is expensive and may be prone to corruption in third-world countries such as ours.

Parliamentary system may be better?

In the Executive, we need to reduce the number of ministers from 42 or so to a maximum of 20. There shouldn't be duplication of ministers as we are operating currently. The number of parastatals should be reduced drastically. Those having similar functions should be merged.

The Legislature is also contributing to the bloated bureaucracy and profligacy. We have 109 Senators and 360 Representatives, giving a total of 469. The bicameral Legislature we are running should be replaced with a unicameral legislature, with a total number of about 200.

3.   **HIGH COST OF GOVERNANCE**

Our politicians are said to be the highest paid in the world. The take home pay for the President,

Vice President, Ministers, Governors and Commissioners is not known. This is not to talk of security votes that run into billions of Naira. The possibility of paying only allowances to politicians should be discussed and implemented. This will limit the political space for those who are going there to serve the people and not their pockets. It will sound reasonable if the President's allowance (not salary) is pegged at the maximum not above the salary of a professor in the University system. Those below the President of course will have an equivalent of Senior Registrar's salary.

4. **CORRUPTION**

The issue of corruption has been discussed in Chapter Two.

5. **FREE AND FAIR ELECTIONS**

Electing the right people free from rigging and pre-election violence should be discussed. To achieve the above, the Electoral body should be truly independent in their appointments and funding. In fact, Justice Uwais Recommendations should be dusted and implemented fully.

6.   **SECTION 308 IMMUNITY CLAUSE**

This should be tabled in the Conference. Clear differentiation should be made between civil and criminal cases. Immunity should be allowed for civil cases only.

7.   **STRONG INSTITUTIONS**

As President Obama said during his visit to Ghana in 2009:

> *In the 21st century, capable,*
> *reliable and transparent*

> ***institutions are the key to success - strong parliaments and honest police forces; independent judges and journalists, a vibrant private sector and civil society. Those are the things that give life to democracy, because that is what matters in people's lives.***

We need strong and independent institutions such as Legislature, Judiciary, the Press, EFCC, ICPC etc.

If the above issues, and many others not yet mentioned, are discussed in a brotherly spirit and sincerely implemented, one Nigeria of our dreams will be realized.

It is the failure or refusal to allow the people come together to discuss their common problems, and right the political wrongs, that can throw the country into more chaos.

HOW WILL THE DELEGATES FOR THE CONFERENCE BE APPOINTED, SELECTED OR ELECTED?

This should not be an impediment to the success of the Conference. Some have suggested a meeting of ethnic nationalities. Opponents of this proposition point to the difficulties of bringing together the more than 300 ethnic nationalities in Nigeria. Some say the ethnic nationalities are even more than 500!

How, they argue, will it be fair to have a major ethnic nationality of population of twenty or forty million people have equal representation with those of minority groups of about five hundred thousand, or even one hundred people?

We can easily solve this seeming problem without splitting hairs! The goal of every patriotic

Nigerian is to have a united country where all will have equal sense of belonging, not minding whether we are in the majority or minority. We can achieve this through general consensus on how best to bring the greatest development to the greatest number of people, under the prism of justice, unity and equity.

Some have suggested that delegates should come from each of the 774 LGAs. This also is perpetuation of the great injustice we will be sitting to correct as distribution of LGAs is skewed.

It is pertinent to allay the fears of the major ethnic nationalities on fair and equitable representation in the NC. Emergence of delegates is expected to be based on the six geo-political regions or zones, selecting or electing equal number of the representatives.

There is no way all of the ethnic nationalities numbering more than three hundred or so can be represented in the NC. The most sensible thing to do is to have a very fair distribution of the ethnic nationalities within each geo-political zone to fit into the specified number of delegates for each zone.

The specified number of delegates of each of the six geo-political zones is a welcome idea, in addition to specified number of representatives from all major stakeholders, given a total number of about five hundred delegates.

The stakeholders will include delegates from the Executive arm of Government, the National Assembly, the Judiciary, the Armed Forces/ Police and other security agents, Nigeria Labour Congress, Traditional Leaders, Civil Society groups, Women's groups, People with Disabilities, Market Men and Women, Nigeria

PROPOSED COMPOSITION OF THE NATIONAL CONFERENCE

S/N	STAKEHOLDERS	DETAILS	DELEGATES	REMARKS
1.	Elder Statesmen	1 per State and FCT	37	Nomination by President
2.	Retired Military and Security Personnel: i. Military ii. Police iii. State Security and NIA	1 per Geo-political Zone 1 per Geo-political Zone 1 per Geo-political Zone	6 6 6	Nomination by Stakeholders
3.	Traditional Rulers	2 per Zone + 1 for FCT	13	Nomination by Stakeholders
4.	Retired Civil Servants	1 per Zone	6	Nomination by Stakeholders
5.	Labour Representatives: i. NLC ii. TUC	Nominations should reflect Geo-political and Gender Balance	12 12	Nomination by NLC Nomination by TUC
6.	Organised Private Sector i. NECA ii. MAN iii. NACCIMA iv. NESG		2 2 2 2	Nomination by Stakeholders
7.	Nigeria Youth Organisations: i. Nat. Youth Council of Nigeria ii. NANS iii. Other (Outstanding Youths and Role Models)	1 per Geo-political Zone 1 per Geo-political Zone 1 per Geo-political Zone	6 6 6	Nomination by Stakeholders Nomination by Stakeholders Nomination by Federal Government
8.	Women Groups: i. NCWS ii. Market Women Associations iii. FIDA, NAWOJ, WINBIZ	2 per Geo-political Zone 1 per Geo-political Zone 2 per Organisation	12 6 6	Nomination by Stakeholders

9.	Political Parties: i. PDP ii. APC iii. APGA iv. Accord Party v. Labour Party	Parties that have representation in the National Assembly	2 2 2 2 2	Nomination by Stakeholders
10.	Muslim Leaders		6	Nomination by Stakeholders
11.	Christian Leaders		6	Nomination by Stakeholders
12.	Civil Society Organisations	Ensure spread	24	Nomination by Stakeholders
13.	Nigerians in Diaspora (Europe, America, Africa, Asia and Middle East)	2 per location	8	Nomination by Stakeholders
14.	People Living with Disabilities	1 per Geo-political Zone	6	Nomination by Stakeholders
15.	Newspapers Proprietors Association of Nigeria		2	Nomination by Stakeholders
16.	Nigeria Guild of Editors		2	Nomination by Stakeholders
17.	Nigeria Union of Journalists		2	Nomination by Stakeholders
18.	Broadcasting Organisation of Nigeria		2	Nomination by Stakeholders
19.	Socio-Political/Cultural and Ethnic Nationality Groups	15 per Geo-political Zone-Nominations should reflect Ethnic and Religious Diversities.	90	Nomination by Stakeholders
20.	Professional Bodies: NBA, NSE, CIB, NMA, NIM, NIA, ICAN, ANAN, NIPR, AAPN, NIESV, Nigerian Environmental Society, Nigeria Economic Society.	1 per Organisation	13	Nomination by Stakeholders

21.	National Academies: 　i.　Academy of Science 　ii.　Academy of Engineering 　iii. Academy of Education 　iv. Academy of Letters 　v.　Academy of Social Sciences	1 per Academy	5	Nomination by Stakeholders
22.	Judiciary	Persons not currently serving on the Bench	6	Nomination by President
23.	Former Political Officeholders: 　i.　Former Governors 　ii.　Senators Forum 　iii. House of Reps. Forum 　iv. Association ofFormer Speakers	1 per Geo political Zone 1 per Geo political Zone 1 per Geo political Zone 1 per Geo political Zone	6 6 6 6	Nomination by Stakeholders
24.	Federal Government of Nigeria	20 at least 6 shall be women	20	Nomination by FGN
25.	State Governments and FCT	3 per State and 1 for FCT		
26.	Former LGA Chairmen	1 per Geo-political Zone	6	Nomination by ALGON
27.	Chairman, Deputy Chair and Secretary	Geo-political spread to be observed	3	Nomination by President

TOTAL NUMBER OF DELEGATES -   492

www.ingramcontent.com/pod-product-compliance
Lightning Source LLC
Chambersburg PA
CBHW050800160726

48004CB00002B/646